# THE POCKETBOOK OF RELATIONSHIPS

Karen Cornell, Jane Li Fox &
Marleen Putnam

FIRST EDITION
First Printing, 2008
Cover design by Linnea Armstrong

Library of Congress Control Number:
Cornell, Karen, Jane Li Fox & Marleen Putnam—
      The Pocketbook of Relationships/
Karen Cornell, Jane Li Fox & Marleen Putnam  1ˢ ed.
        p.       cm.
        Includes bibliographical references.
        ISBN:978-0-9797906-1-4
If you wish to contact the authors or would like more information about this book, please contact the authors in care of Triple Eight Publishing and we will forward your request.

Karen Cornell, Jane Li Fox & Marleen Putnam
Mountlake Terrace, WA

**pocketbook3@gmail.com**

# CONTENTS

PART FOUR - The Straw That Broke the
Camel's Back (Turning Points)

PART FIVE - I've Made my Bed, Now How do I
Lie in it? (Solutions and Resolutions)

## Acknowledgement

When faced with a problem, find a solution. We are so blessed to have found Linnea Armstrong when we needed her. Her abilities and creativity, coupled with her knowledge of the publishing and printing worlds, have been invaluable to novices like us. She is tenacious in problem-solving and patient with those of us who are still learning. Kudos to Linnea and a big thank you from the bottom of our hearts.

— The Authors

# INTRODUCTION

If any of our friends knew we three were writing a book on relationships, they would fall on the floor laughing! All of us have been divorced (some of us more than once). We have had some spectacularly awful relationships and currently, being single is looking good to all three of us!  None of that sounds like much of a recommendation for authoring a book on relationships does it? But that is precisely the point. We are not counselors or psychologists. We are students of life and our collective experiences, and what we have learned, may be of help to those of you struggling with relationship issues.

So sit back and relax while we share with you what we know, what we don't know, what we think we know and what we don't ever want to experience again! We learned it all the hard way. Hopefully you will gain from our mistakes.

# Part One

## From Diapers to Driving (Those Early Relationships)

*This part is about the personal relationships that affect you as you are growing up and how they form your ways of thinking, who you are, and how you relate to others in your relationships later in life.*

# 1

## FAMILY RELATIONSHIPS

Did you ever feel like the stork lost his way in a storm and dropped you into the wrong family? We've probably all felt that way at one time or another.

The fact is, early relationships with parents, siblings, grandparents, aunts, uncles and cousins create the basis for who we are and how we relate to people. If you grew up in a family where people communicated with each other, you are probably going to be a fairly good communicator. If you grew up in a family that was positive and laughed a lot and expressed unconditional love, you are probably a pretty joyful and happy person.

Unfortunately, for many of us, that was not the case. Early negative life experiences have sent scores of us to therapists to try and untangle the damage done (often unwittingly) by our well-meaning families. Many times, as children, we develop misconceptions about family dynamics that affect our thought patterns as we grow older. Whether or not the memories we carry are accurate, they affect how we relate to others as well as how we see ourselves. Of course, there could have been extenuating circumstances, which we will address in a later chapter.

But the bottom line is, few of us have had a perfect childhood. Where we go with it, and what we do with it, is what we want to address in this book.

## 2

### EXTENDED FAMILY AND FRIENDS

Just what is "extended family"? We feel it refers to people in our lives who "feel" like family even though they may not be blood relatives. These people could be next-door neighbors or they may be acquired through divorce and re-marriage (such as stepparents, stepbrothers and sisters) or they could be school friends. You are fortunate if you have experienced these relationships as major blessings in your life.

However, we understand that this is not the case for everyone. Some extended relationships are really challenging. All three of us can attest to that! These relationships play a major role in who we are and who we become.

First, let's address friendships. As a young child, your friends will often have a bigger influence on you than your parents. Some of our friends may have had a positive influence, but others probably led us down primrose lane! The ones who led you down primrose lane and used you were not really your friends. The ones who supported you and were loyal and honest are worthy to be called friends.

Unfortunately, as young children we usually don't have the ability to recognize the difference between a negative influence and a positive influence. And if we don't have a strong influential base at home to show us the way (and some of us didn't), we are totally confused.

Those negative friendships as children can be the basis for what turns into low self-esteem later in life. Hopefully, you learned to "weed your garden" so that as an adult, you know the difference between a true friend and a passing acquaintance.

Death or divorce (and/or subsequent re-marriage) brings on a whole different set of experiences. First of all, you have a sense of abandonment brought on by the absence of one parent, whether or not it was that parent's idea. Any time a family unit is broken, it will create a feeling of abandonment. And sometimes, a child will take on the responsibility for the death or divorce. "I must have done something wrong" enters into the child's thinking.

This is really hard to overcome as you get older. If there is no strong influence from somewhere (family member or friend) to help you understand the situation, it may become an excuse later in life for not taking responsibility for your life and your decisions.

If there is remarriage, then there are step-parents and maybe stepsiblings involved. This can be a pleasant experience or an unpleasant one, depending on the people involved. If it is pleasant, great! If not, wow! That is stuff you carry with you forever. At some point down the road, you will have to make a conscious deci-sion to let go of all the negatives and deal with your own life without blaming your problems on your stepmother, stepfather, stepsiblings, and so forth.

Adoption is another area where abandon-ment comes into play. The adopted child, even though he or she may have wonderful adoptive parents, often has a desire or need to know why he was given up in the first place. If no answers are available, the child may once again take on the responsibility for being given up.

"I wasn't wanted," "I wasn't loved," or "I did something wrong" are perceptions about the situation — not necessarily fact. But the number of adopted adults looking for their original parents in today's world bears out the fact that abandonment issues still exist in their perception.

The point of this discussion is that those experiences that we have with extended family carry over into adulthood. And unless we are very lucky, they can lead to a sense of low self-esteem and real neediness.

Neediness comes in two forms. Neither is very pretty and neither has the ingredients for successful relationships.

One form of neediness comes out in real "need." I "need" someone to make me whole, take care of me, save me, etc. The other form shows as a person who must "be needed." — "Who am I if no one needs me?" There are even those who suffer from both! The person who needs to be needed may, as a parent for instance, influence their children in such a way that the children become completely dependent on the parent and cannot fend for themselves. The person who needs someone else in their life to feel complete may ultimately endanger any potential relationship by smothering the other person. This applies to friendships as well as to intimate relationships.

All of the things we have just discussed can be changed and overcome. So don't give up, dear friends. There is light at the end of the tunnel!

*There is nothing standing between you and the person you want to be—except your own fears!*

## 3

### INFLUENCE OF RELIGION

Religious training often begins very early in life, even before a child starts elementary school. Small children, even toddlers, are put into Sunday school while Mommy and Daddy attend church.

No matter what the basic belief system is, a small child is very impressionable. What children learn at this age may well influence their attitudes for life. If the influence is a positive one, future relationships and experiences may be more pleasant than if the influence is negative. A child's perception, be it right or wrong, is what is carried into adult life. Religious leaders, because they are usually presented as good and powerful, also have a huge influence on children.

In any situation, not just church and religion, if we allow the views and beliefs of a powerful person or organization to take over our thinking, that is when we begin to give up our personal sense of responsibility. This creates a comfort zone where we feel accepted into a community that as we grow older, we may be reluctant to leave.  As we have said, the feelings of abandonment are strong and will keep us in situations and relationships long after we should have moved on.

# 4

## The "Wonder" Years

From the time we enter elementary school till the day we leave high school, we are totally and completely bombarded with every kind of influence imaginable!

In today's world, kids are faced with choices that can seem impossible. First of all, kids need to be accepted by their peers. They also need to feel their own power to step out and make decisions for themselves. That need can lead to making a choice about doing drugs, being in a gang, carrying a gun *or* being a good student, participating in social activities such as clubs and sports, and striving for higher achievements. These are the years that are going to lead them to what they are as adults. It's a "wonder" any of us survived!

## In Conclusion ...

We would like to finish this section with words of encouragement. We have all had our own sets of problems and experiences as children and teenagers. What each of us does with those experiences will set the tone in our relationships as we go forward with our lives.

Remember, your sense of humor will get you everywhere!

Laugh often. It's good for ya'!

# Part Two

## From Idealist to Realist (Grown-Up Relationships)

*This section is not just about marriage. It is about committed relationships of all kinds: marriage, significant others, etc.*

# 1

## FRIENDSHIPS

When we are young, teens through our twenties, we tend to be very idealistic. We see the world and the people in our lives through rose-colored glasses.

On the last day of high school, didn't you sign yearbooks and promise to be "friends forever"? And then three or four years later, you suddenly realize there are a whole bunch of friends that you haven't seen or heard from since graduation.

What happened? You moved forward on your own path, living your own life, and not all of those friends were going in the same direction as you. Nor did you fit into their lives.

Through each phase of our lives, we meet people, make friends and grow because of those friendships. When we have learned all we can from each other, we move on.

The trick is to know when a friendship has served its purpose and then to be brave enough to let it go. Cherish the memories of old friendships, realizing that "friendship" lasts forever—the faces just change.

*Follow the Three "Rs":*
*Respect for self*
*Respect for others*
*Responsibility for all*
*your actions.*

## 2

### RESPONSIBILITY IN RELATIONSHIPS

Basically, all friendships are relationships, whether brief or ongoing. Any relationship brings with it responsibility on the part of both parties. It takes "two to tango," so to speak. Within the realm of responsibility falls the need to be non-judgmental.

One of the quickest ways to ruin any relationship is to be judgmental. Some of us judge people on appearance, color, gender, religion, politics and any number of things. The interesting thing is we tend to see other people as we see ourselves. So when we criticize someone for the way they look, or what they believe, we generally are not too happy with ourselves in those areas.

In our previous book, *The Pocketbook of Prosperity, Peace and Personal Power*, we discussed the subject of energy. Energy goes out and collects "like" energy. What you focus on is what you get. If you focus on a negative experience, you will have a negative experience. If you focus on the negative attributes of your friend or partner, your friend or partner will give you more of the same!

Stop focusing on the negative and start focusing on the positive things you want to see in your relationships. Nurturing a relationship means giving love, attention and acceptance to the other person, and allowing the other person to do the same for you. Nurturing a relationship means letting go of right or wrong, good or bad, and only expecting the highest and the best that each of you can give. When you can do that, you will find all of your relationships moving to a new and wonderful level.

## 3

### THE LAW OF ATTRACTION
### (A DEADLY THING—
### AT LEAST FOR SOME OF US!)

In discussing this subject, we agreed on one
thing: we are attracted to a person by outward
characteristics, such as looks, smile, personality,
etc. Those are the superficial things that make us
want to get to know the person better.

Hot on the heels of this attraction comes
"lust," and oh, dear readers, trust us on this
one. Tread lightly! Lust is a cover-up for many
things, good sense being one of them! People
have the tendency to get married in "lust," not in
"love."

We often mistake lust for love, which means
we don't take the time to look past the outer
shell to see what the inner person is like. Looks
can be deceiving. What you "see" is not necessarily what you get. It is important to take the
time to become "friends" with a person.

This is where you really learn about what
a person thinks and feels and believes in. And
it may not be what *you* think or feel or believe
in. This person may make a great acquaintance,

but not a great partner, and you need to take the time to find that out.

The issue we are skirting around here is that hopping into bed right away might not be the best idea! Sex brings in a plethora of emotions on both sides and if you haven't taken the time to really get to know each other, you are going to be totally unprepared to deal with them.

A sexual (or intimate) relationship instantly brings with it responsibilities. If you have not examined how *you* feel about intimate relationships, or what your needs are, or what the other person's needs are, you can end up on the outside looking in and wondering what just happened. It's like making the touchdown before the kick-off!

The problem here is the difference in emotional make-up between men and women. Women are generally very right-brained and emotional, and sex is a very emotional experience for them. Men are much more left-brained and pragmatic (kind of the Mr. Spock logical type) and tend to view sex as a happy experience and pastime.

This is why we say, take the time to become friends, talk, share ideas, communicate with one another, so you know you are on the same page before beginning something as intimate as a sexual relationship.

26

And speaking of communication, let's talk about the difference in communication styles between men and women. Our experience is that unless one of the parties has some really highly developed communication skills, they don't hear each other and there is no point of understanding. We need a point of understanding to create a common meeting ground when we talk to each other.

Men tend to see things in black and white. Women see things in many shades of varying colors. They need to "hear" they are loved and appreciated. They need the flowers, the hugs, the candy, the dinner out, the weekend alone. Whether or not that seems fair to their men, that is the way it is.

Men feel they show their love by being the providers or mowing the lawn. They feel that just "being there" shows you that they love you. To them, "actions speak louder than words." But women really do need the words. The trick is for them to be able to let their men "know" what they need and for their men to "hear" them.

Sound complicated? It doesn't have to be. Communication is everything. With a little practice you can both learn to speak the language of the heart.

*Let your heart be your guide.*
*You must listen carefully,*
*as it whispers.*
*Are you listening to your heart?*

# 4

## DIFFERENCE IN INTERESTS

From the time a baby is born, he or she is steered in a direction of interest by parents, grandparents, religious teachers, academic teachers, friends and the big one—media advertising!

If you are a girl, everything is pink and Barbie. There are little kitchens, little carpet sweepers, paper dolls, doll houses, and so forth—anything to steer them toward being the "housewife" when they grow up.

Boy toys tend to be trucks and cars, tool sets, lawn mowers, guns (lately laser guns), soldiers and everything macho. There are some crossover toys like Legos, but the girls tend to build houses and the boys build army forts!

If a girl wants to climb a tree, she is a "tomboy." If a boy wants to sit down and play "dolls" or "house" with his sister, he is a "sissy." While there is more latitude for crossover in activities in today's children, there still seems to be some stigma attached to the idea that a girl might like to race cars or a boy might like to cook.

The harm in this division of interests comes in the later years when, as adults, you are trying to form a relationship with the opposite sex and find that you have no common interests. We do see that in the present generation, there is less division of interests along gender lines than there used to be, but the trick in a relationship is appreciating each others' differences.

The appreciation must be accompanied by a willingness to allow each person to be themselves and enjoy their activities of choice. There also needs to be a willingness to share each others' activities: "I'll do this with you if you will do that with me." Or appreciate your differences and allow each of you to have a "personal" day: "You do that and I will go do this. Meet you back here for dinner." It's a matter of caring about each other enough and trusting each other enough to share the things you want to share and to do other things separately without feeling threatened.

How important is it to have things in common? It is very important. But it is equally important to allow each other to be the individuals you have always been. Few relationships can stand 24/7 togetherness. Give each other space when necessary and you will appreciate your together times that much more.

# 5

## ACHIEVING JOY AND HAPPINESS
## IN A RELATIONSHIP

We're really out in left field here since none of the three of us have ever achieved joy and happiness in our relationships, at least not in marriage! Now friendships are a different thing. We all have wonderful friends, both men and women. But, for better or worse, we are here to discuss personal, intimate and loving relationships between two people.

**Point One:** A relationship with another person will only be as good as the relationship you have with yourself. If you are insecure or jealous or demanding, you are going to doom a relationship before it ever gets off the ground. You need to know what you are willing to give and what you are willing to receive in a relationship. And you need to present yourself as you really are. Putting up a "good front" to impress another person will take you right down the yellow brick road. Honesty is always the best policy for the basis of a relationship.

**Point Two:** There are no silk purses here! Nobody is perfect. "Perfect" doesn't exist, at least not in humans. So letting go of expectations in a relationship is the key to its survival. (Note: tears from the three of us on this one!)

The minute you "expect" a certain thing from another person, you set yourself up for disappointment. Expectations are unfair because what you want is only in your head and the other person can't read your mind. You need to know what you want, be clear about it and communicate it! And this needs to be a two-way street. Both of you need to come from a point of honesty and integrity for a relationship to even begin, let alone survive and thrive.

**Point Three:** If you think you are going to change your partner, you have another think coming! Remember the line, "for better or for worse"? Well get ready to deal with what you consider the "worse" part. None of us are really going to change. What was okay before we "tied the knot" suddenly isn't okay at all. For example, holes in the jeans were "cute" before marriage and "make him look like a bum" after marriage. For his part, he doesn't know why the holes in the jeans are bad since that is what he has been wearing all along. For her part, it seems like a reflection on her if her mate looks bad.

Suddenly, the fact that she talks to her mother every day, which was an endearing and sweet and caring quality before, becomes annoying because she is always on the phone.

Now we have a battle going on about changing each other. Dear friends, this is a fruitless battle with no winners. Nagging and criticism only add to the problem. The minute criticism comes into play, then resistance from the criticized party is set up. From here comes the standoff which often leads to out-and-out war.

Do you see where we are going with this? There is no "winning" in this war and no "changing the other person." There is really only one answer here, folks, and that is "acceptance." When we learn to accept the other person as he /she is and appreciate all of the wonderful qualities that person has, and to ignore the "warts," then the relationship can grow and be wonderful. If all you want to focus on is the toothpaste tube squeezed in the middle, you will squeeze the life right out of the relationship and doom it to failure.

**Point Four:** You can only make *yourself* happy. Contrary to popular belief, it is not the responsibility of your mate to make you happy. Nor is it your responsibility to make your mate happy. However, we are taught from the cradle that we must have a mate and then make him or her happy in order to keep them.

You know what? You can't even give someone a case of measles unless you have them yourself first! So how can you be expected to make someone else happy unless you know how to make yourself happy? Creating for yourself the environment that brings to you all of the things that make you happy is your responsibility. And remember what we said about expectations in Point Two? If you "expect" someone to "make you happy," disappointment is probably on its way.

Creating a relationship based on "being saved" or needing the relationship to bring you "money and security" or expecting someone to "take over your responsibilities" sends the other person into a tailspin trying to meet your needs. This creates a communication gap that eventually cannot be bridged.

## In Conclusion ...

We encourage you to take responsibility for your happiness and encourage your mate to do the same. Then, your relationship will be built on a strong foundation.

*Trying to master others makes you vulnerable. Mastering yourself makes you fearless!*

# PART THREE

## BREAKING THE MOLD (DIVERSITY IN RELATIONSHIPS)

*In this section we would like to address the many different types of loving and intimate relationships.*

# 1

## KARMIC RELATIONSHIPS
## (LEARNING THE HARD WAY!)

Whether or not you believe in karma really doesn't matter. What it means is "as you sow, so shall you reap." In other words, "whatever you put out into the Universe is what you will get back."

Karmic relationships almost always involve some kind of lesson for one or both parties And have you ever noticed how the same lesson keeps presenting itself to you over and over and over again? It is what we call being a slow learner!

You may have already asked the question, "why does this keep happening to me?" However, the real question should be, "what am I doing to keep attracting this experience to me?"

Karmic relationships are repetitions of experience. The people may change, but the experiences are the same. Why is that? It is because *you* are not changing your perception of your role in the relationship.

You keep blaming your partner or the circumstances or your parents or your job for things not going right. The truth of the matter is you need to look at yourself and what you believe about relationships.

Many of us have a series of "programs" that we replay over and over again, just like the reruns on TV. And just like the reruns on TV, we only watch the ones we like! We keep creating the same set of circumstances with every new person we meet, because it is familiar and comfortable ... at least for a while, anyway.

The first step in breaking this pattern is recognizing your role in your relationship failures. This may not be an easy thing to do, as we all want to be right.

The problem is we continue to attract to us people who are as damaged as we are. If you are insecure, you will attract an insecure person. If you must have a mate to feel whole, again you will attract that kind of mate. If you are needy, you will attract someone who is needy. Changing your view of what a relationship is, what you want in a relationship, and what your role in a relationship is has to be done in order to change the relationship you attract.

If you have read our previous book, *The Pocketbook of Prosperity, Peace and Personal Power* (and the first two chapters of *this* book), we have been telling you that how you think, what you put out to the Universe with your thoughts, words and actions is what you will get back. You need to identify what you want in a relationship, and have that be your point of focus. If you want a mate that is kind, you need to be prepared to be kind in return. If you want a mate that is funny or knows how to carry on a conversation, you better be prepared to communicate and laugh! What you are prepared to give is what you will receive.

There is an old adage that says the "past does not equal the future," which is true unless we are unwilling to change. We can go along forever living the same unfulfilling relationships or we can face the music, take the bull by the horns, break the mold, and change ourselves so that our future relationships will be joyful and lasting.

Ghandi said, "We must become the change we want to see." The choice is yours.

*How are you doing with
your relationships?
Are you too proud to admit it
when you're wrong?*

## 2

## GAY AND LESBIAN RELATIONSHIPS

Because we live in a part of the United States with the largest gay and lesbian population next to San Francisco, we felt it was necessary to address this subject.

All three of us have known gay and lesbian couples in highly successful and long-term relationships. We have also known gay and lesbian couples who were in difficult, unsuccessful relationships. However, the reasons for their success or failure are the same as those that cause heterosexual relationships to fail or succeed. To this point in our book, we have already talked in great measure about what makes or breaks a relationship, so we won't belabor those issues further.

What we have found is that gay people don't have the same limitations in their thinking as we do. The misconception in our society that a loving environment can only be created by heterosexual couples often leads to a judgmental attitude. The loving and caring in a relationship is what is important because being judgmental doesn't work in any relationship.

There are many examples in today's world of gay people—many of them celebrities—who are highly successful, living within, and raising families within, a loving and caring home and relationship. We would all do well to adopt a "live and let live" attitude and appreciate each and every person for who they are and what they are contributing, not only to society, but to our planet as a whole.

# 3

## Race Differences
## (honoring those differences)

Thirty years ago, seeing a couple of two different races was rare, and usually brought comments from others ending in non-acceptance. Today, seeing couples of mixed races is very common.

What is it that makes these relationships successful? It is the same thing that makes any relationship successful: acceptance of each other! They each focus on what is wonderful about the other person. It behooves all of us to do the same.

There is a lesson to be learned here. First, we must accept ourselves as we are before we can accept others as they are. Nothing is as it appears. Recognizing the level of love and commitment between two people far surpasses outer appearances.

For many of us it is necessary to go within and examine our old programming and find the strength to change it. If we can do that, we have taken a giant step toward acceptance and appreciation of *all* loving couples, and that is where we all need to be.

*If you want to build a
wonderful relationship, be
prepared to give up the
pride and prejudices
that hold you back.*

# 4

## Reproduction Issues
## (the "clock is ticking" syndrome)

In today's world, "reproduction" is no longer just an act of God. It has become a catalyst for much happiness but also for all sorts of battles. In deciding to have a child, one of the first discussions needs to be whether or not both people involved want one! Is the time right? Is the relationship strong enough to support parenthood? How many children do both of you want? How many can you afford? (That one is really important.)

Be mindful that in a new relationship, when lust rides high, people don't always tell the truth. They say whatever the other person wants to hear. Or the other person doesn't hear what is really being said. We have a tendency to gloss over issues of major importance at that stage of the game.

And speaking of games, we also have "the blame game." Whose fault is it that we are not pregnant? Or, whose fault is it that we are pregnant and would rather not be? Either of these issues brings about all kinds of resentment because it indicates one of you is imperfect or one of you is careless. Obviously this breeds distrust, but that is "the blame game." It is easier for the problems to be somebody else's fault.

Responsibility is a huge issue for many men. They are looking at 18-20 years of care and support, both financially and emotionally. But the motherhood instinct is so strong in some women that they don't look at what it is going to take to raise this child until they have already had a child or children. Then the reality check sets in for both parents. Now they may be feeling trapped, but there is no going back.

Other problems are created when a woman traps a man into marriage by purposely getting pregnant. Or, when one partner insists on being married but the other partner feels trapped by marriage.

Programming from childhood has played a key role in how relationships are conducted. When you are raised in a cultural or religious atmosphere that demands certain things (such as a man demanding that his wife have a child even though she doesn't want to, or a man wanting only a boy and then blaming his wife when it is a girl), it puts undue and unfair pressure on the relationship. It takes a long time before we are mature enough to look past someone else's thinking and make our own decisions.

So what are the answers to these problems? We see two very important solutions. The first is communication with honesty. We cannot emphasize this enough. Without honest communication from both parties there are no solutions.

The second is accepting responsibility for your own decisions and realizing that the answers to the dilemmas you have created may not be exactly the ones you want to hear.

## In Conclusion ...

Look in the mirror and recognize your role in this relationship. Be willing to examine, discuss, go for counseling or do whatever it takes to resolve the problems.

Are you willing to do this?

*Be to yourself what you would love to have in another person.*

# PART FOUR

# THE STRAW THAT BROKE THE CAMEL'S BACK (TURNING POINTS)

*In this section we would like to address the challenges relationships face as the years roll on. These are the points that can make or break a relationship.*

# 1

## INDEPENDENCE VERSUS DEPENDENCE

If each of us had a strong sense of self-esteem and a clear idea of who we are, most of the things we are writing about would not be an issue—and we wouldn't be writing this book!

But we are taught at a very young age to give our power away because we want to please our parents, our friends or our teachers. We want to be liked by everyone! The trick is to raise a child with kindness and teach them the proper social attitudes without breaking their spirit and sending their self-esteem into the basement.

How often does this happen? Not often enough, unfortunately. For most of us, the minute we get into a relationship, we seem to immediately give up our own ideas and dreams to make the other person "happy." What is honest about that? Absolutely nothing.

The problem with this scenario is that by the time you get five, ten or fifteen years down the road, you realize that the life you have created didn't include you! Wow! Does this ever create a "resentment" factor!

It is important that from the beginning each person in the relationship is recognized as an individual and appreciated for what each of you brings to the table.

This brings us to the subject of trying to "change" your partner. When you judge your mate, you are saying that he or she is not adequate the way they are. When you concentrate on changing someone else, you are not looking at the changes you need to make in yourself. Essentially what you are conveying is, "everything that is wrong with this relationship is your fault so we need to change you."

This rarely works. (And we know because all three of us have tried it!) Acceptance is the key here. If you liked this person well enough to be together in the first place, what changed? Did the person change or did your perception of the person change?

Be honest. Are you dissatisfied with your mate or are you dissatisfied with yourself? The only person you can really change is you. Better start there.

Control issues are another "hot button" in relationships. Why is it that one person feels they must dominate the other? Fear is usually at the bottom of it. Being in control gives one a false sense of power and security. We are here to tell you that dominance in a relationship gets you nowhere fast! The choice is, do you want to be loved or do you want to be right? We are once again pointing out that accepting each other for all your good qualities (the ones you saw in each other in the first place) and accepting that neither of you is perfect is the only way any relationship will work.

We are all capable of creating the life we want for ourselves, whether in a relationship or not. Your voice is your power. Whatever you say is what you will manifest. Say it kindly to both yourself and your mate.

*Being Captain of your own ship is essential to a healthy relationship. Just be sure your ship is going in the right direction!*

## 2

### MONEY AND CHILDREN IN A RELATIONSHIP (BOTH CAN BE DEADLY!)

We would like to point out that the subjects of money and children are something we shouldn't even have to discuss here, because they should have been discussed long *before* you ever decided to become serious about your relationship.

However, almost no one ever discusses these things in depth at the beginning of the relationship (love is blind, etc.). So months or years down the road, battle lines are often drawn over the two most critical subjects in any marriage/relationship.

Money is an "energy" that we use to attain the goods and services that we need. Long ago this was accomplished with a bartering system. But in today's world, we use cold, hard cash, and in today's world we are bombarded by the media with things that we "must have" to be happy. It is no wonder then that couples often find themselves deeply in debt.

Our alternative to cold hard cash has become credit cards, and the credit card companies are only too willing to keep us in debt up to our eyebrows!

Now, there isn't a couple in the world who won't have problems when the outgo far surpasses the income. There may be one partner who is ultra-practical, wants everything defined and in order, needs to know that the required amount of money is coming each month to cover the amount going out each month. But the other partner may see things more as "everything will be okay" and doesn't think in terms of definite numbers. This is where trouble begins. Judgment sets in and war begins and this is the start of a huge trust issue.

We have been told that money truly is the root of all evil and it brings out the worst in all of us. Rather, we think that each person's perception of money, and the role it plays in their lives, is the true problem.

If the two of you don't view money the same way, there is no way the relationship can be healthy. Without honesty, communication and discussion about this issue, you cannot create a secure foundation for the relationship to survive. (And as we have said, this should have been discussed before and not ten or twenty years down the road!)

If you get to this point, there are options available to you to help resolve some of your money issues. There are financial planners and counselors available to you if you can afford them. There are great books you can buy on budgeting. If nothing more, there are some good TV shows and tapes you can watch that will teach you some of the basics of money management.

However, the most important point here is that you find a common meeting ground upon which to focus and work out your differences. We've said it before and we say it again: what you think about is what you create. If both of you will think about being prosperous and abundant, you will be. If you want prosperity in your lives, and if you are willing to work together to achieve it, it will happen. If you work against each other, kiss it all goodbye!

On the subject of children, please reread the above section on money. It all applies! But since we are writing this book, and we love to talk, we will elaborate on the subject.

Before you decide to have a permanent relationship with a person, you need to know what their compassion level is. Does this person like animals? Does this person like kids? Does this person even like your friends? Moreover, do your friends like this person? Do you have enough common ground to build a relationship that, should it lead to a family, it is going to create a good atmosphere for raising children? If you are with a person who doesn't like animals much, and doesn't like people much, and doesn't like your friends and they don't like him/her either, and this person doesn't like kids, what are you thinking if you are a person who wants to have a family?

Ah, but when new love is all dewy and wonderful, we are all oh so willing to ignore these red flags because we think we know what we want. (I just know I can change him/her). The old adage is, "Let's point the canoe upstream and do it the hard way!" Where do children fit in to this scenario? We have one person who wants them and one person who does not. A recipe for disaster.

Oh well, too late. The children are already here. Now we have to find a way to agree on raising the little buggers! When you add another person to the mix, especially in "tiny" form, it will magnify other issues that already existed, be they financial or emotional. What used to be red flags are now real problems.

Children at any age need a lot of attention and direction. The parents must agree on how to administer the education, discipline and, most of all, love and security to promote the well-being of the child. This is hard with one child and sometimes almost impossible with several children.

Fighting between the parents about issues such as money choices, emotional neglect, and how to discipline the children leaves everyone exhausted and drained and creates an unhappy atmosphere for the entire family. The children will often think they are responsible for these problems.

It is at this point that couples may decide to stay together for the sake of the children. This is not necessarily a good idea without professional counseling. These problems are bigger than both of you. It is time to set aside your own ego and look at the bigger picture if you want your marriage/relationship and family to stay intact.

*Wealth is a mindset and it can come in many forms. And the form is not always "money." Recognizing and appreciating what you have is essential in a good and loving relationship.*

## 3

### THINGS NO ONE WANTS TO TALK ABOUT (BUT EVERYBODY SHOULD!)

For all of you out there who are secure within yourselves, this part is not for you. However, if jealousy and competition for attention are traits you recognize in yourself (and be honest with yourselves here) then you need to read on.

There are different kinds of jealousy. There is the more superficial kind that comes from being insecure within yourself. This kind bristles when the person you are with pays attention to someone else. The deeper kind of jealousy really has to do with trust and abandonment issues. When you suffer from abandonment issues, you usually expect the other person to rescue you or take care of you. You are also looking for the other person to always be there for you. The fact is, you can only be there for yourself!

That is a hard pill to swallow because you really would like to blame someone else for how you feel. You need to become more introspective about your own feelings. Granted, you are sometimes given reason to not trust what your partner is doing, but jealousy is not the answer. Facing the facts and confronting the issue and talking is the answer. (And that is the hard part!) However, it becomes easier when each person is willing to take responsibility for their actions. And that isn't easy either, but you gotta' do it! This kind of communication enables both parties to look at themselves within the situation, examine their motives and figure out why they are butting heads.

This leads us to the sister subject: the "competition for attention syndrome," which may be the cause of the jealousy in the first place! We live in a society where competition is not only the norm, but is encouraged and expected in our daily lives. We always seem to be trying to "keep up with the Joneses." This is not necessarily a good thing in relationships. It might be a great thing in the business world, but it doesn't add a lot when trying to solidify a cohesive relationship. Learning to appreciate yourself, and then your partner, allows each of you to bring something to the table.

It is not our intent to solve your problems with this book. This book is to bring to your attention emotions and feelings that get in the way of happy and productive relationships. Relationships are meant to be joyful. It is up to you to take all the steps possible to repair the differences that you find in your relationships. We've all been there and we've all had to do it!

The most important step is communication. You have reached the point in your relationship where there is no room for spectators. You must both be participators in making this union work. And please, remember that communication requires both talking and listening.

If you don't get the lines of communication open, then there is the danger that one or both partners will simply give up on the whole thing. Once they have given up, that leads to boredom, which then often leads to cheating and infidelity. That little gal pulling espresso down at the coffee shop looks pretty good, doesn't she? And that hunk down at the gym—woohoo!

Now folks, we want to tell you: if you thought you had problems before, just get involved with one of these situations and **wow**! You ain't seen nothin' yet! On top of a huge lack of communication, you now have lying, sneaking, deceiving, hiding and a whopping big dose of guilt! Life becomes much more complicated and ever more difficult to correct.

Both partners in a relationship that has reached this point must step back and take stock of their own responsibility in this situation.

If they are willing to do this, it could create grounds for a great healing between them.
If not, it's pretty much all over but the shouting.

Of course, there is one more option. And that is staying together because of religion, money, security, the children and any number of other excuses. This option shows clearly that neither party is willing to take "personal responsibility," and that they are just "willing to settle." In our opinion, this option never brings peace, harmony or happiness to either party, because then turmoil and unspoken feelings exist for the rest of their lives.

Which of these options you choose is clearly up to you.

# 4

## How to Know When or If it is Time to Move On

Not all relationships were meant to be "forever." We all come together for a purpose. Each of us has something to learn, and when that has been accomplished, we move on.

A great poet wrote, "We come together for a reason, a season or a lifetime." The trick is to know when the time is over. Because of our programming, we have been taught to feel guilt over this subject, so we tend to hang on to something long after its expiration date!

The ideal partnership is one where two people are growing in the same direction with similar interests and a lot in common. There are many times when people find themselves growing in conflicting directions and losing common meeting ground. This kind of thing needs to be discussed and put out in the open between the two people in order for there to be an intelligent decision about the relationship. You both need to realize that the commonality you once shared may be shifting and you find yourselves uncomfortable in a once comfortable relationship.

Enter fear! None of us likes to "rock the boat" because it takes away our comfort zone. In this case, the fear of being "alone" looms large. Factors involved in the fear of being alone range from financial to emotional. The financial pressures are often the ones people look at first. Setting up two households and supporting both of them, especially if there are children involved, can become formidable. (Even if there are two incomes.)

Another reason couples stay together in the face of conflict are the children. If it is decided that you are staying together for "the sake of the children," then we strongly encourage you to seek counseling. In our opinion, if you have a great deal of conflict and fighting going on in the relationship, it can sometimes do more damage to the children than if you just break it up now and move on. May we add that in order for the counseling to be beneficial, both partners must be willing to accept their share of responsibility for the current state of affairs, and each must also be willing to do their part to create a new set of circumstances that will be of benefit to the whole family.

If you are thinking of breaking up your relationship, look at it honestly to be sure you have done everything you could to make it work.

When you have exhausted all possibilities, and you see no other recourse, you will at least move on guilt-free, knowing you did your part and tried everything to fix the situation. This is not to say you won't have some strong emotions. Breaking up something that once was "wonder-ful" is never easy.

## In Conclusion ...

We have presented you with an abundance of problems and possibilities. Read on and we will try to present you with some ideas for solutions. Bear in mind, we are human too and we might not have the right solution for you.

*To "let go" is not to regret the past, but to grow and live for the future.*

# PART FIVE

## I've Made my Bed, Now How do I Lie in It? (Solutions and Resolutions)

*So now let's get to the good stuff! In this part, we would like to present some positive ideas for turning your relationship back into the fun and loving one it used to be.*

# 1

## "Settling For" Instead of Expecting the Best

You can have your cake and eat it too! We have consistently said to you that what you focus on is what you will create. If you settle for crumbs, you're going to get only crumbs, and the whole cake will never show up!

Settling for something less than what you really desire in a partner is a choice. This can be a conscious choice or an unconscious choice on your part, so it behooves you to spend some time analyzing what it is you want in a relationship. It is too easy to do what your parents want or follow what your friends are doing. Rarely will other people's choices be right for you.

Sit down and make a list of what you want in a long-term, lasting relationship. You will be amazed at what you suddenly won't "settle for."

For those of you who may feel that you have already "settled for," it is not too late to sit down and make that list. You may find that you have more than you thought you had. Or, you may have created a list of things that you and your partner need to discuss. Open discussion with each other makes it possible for your partner to know what you really want and opens the doors for change that can be made by both parties. This kind of interaction can only benefit the relationship. (No screaming matches allowed!)

## 2

### FINDING SOLUTIONS TO THE IRRITATIONS (DON'T SWEAT THE SMALL STUFF!)

Loving and lasting relationships are based on acceptance of one another. This acceptance exists because of love, trust, loyalty, friendship, humor and understanding of one another—all the "big stuff."

The irritating stuff comes in when we are actually trying to live together. We get up in the morning, try to share a bathroom, get ready for work, grab some coffee, get dressed and find that not only are we in each other's way, but we don't do things the same way at all! We are tired, rushed and cranky and tend to let all of the little things get blown way out of proportion.

We would like to point out that if your focus is on irritations, there will be more irritations (like the toilet seat left up or the toothpaste tube squeezed in the middle). But if you focus on each other's positive attributes that attracted you in the first place, those will increase as well.

There are some things, of course, that we simply need to learn to live with. If your partner snores, get ear plugs! If your partner leaves dirty clothes on the floor, put a basket in the corner and ask him/her to practice their best basketball shots! If dishes are left in the sink, instead of being loaded into the dishwasher, use paper plates. If you can't stand using paper plates, then you need to decide what irritates you more, the sink full of dishes or the paper plates. It's your choice! None of the above situations are worth driving yourself nuts over. And none of those are important enough to create a big problem in your relationship.

Appreciation always gets positive results, so don't forget to tell your partner why you love him/her. If you express positive appreciation for someone, you will get positive results in return. This applies to all relationships, from acquaintances and friendships to partnerships.

# 3
## Keeping Romance Alive

In discussing this subject, we found that all three of us had some fun and creative ideas but that many of them would be censored by our publisher! What we do want to do is encourage you to come up with your own creative ideas that will keep the spark ignited between you and your partner.

It is important to a long-term relationship to maintain the fun and spontaneity that existed when you first got together. We have a tendency to let the mundane everyday stuff get in the way, and we forget that the whole secret to a relationships success is to maintain that little sense of fun and intimacy between you.

Remember that we are talking about romance, which is a different subject than sex. Sex is the end result of a good romance.

Romance is knowing what tickles your partner's funny bone. It is remembering to do the nice things for each other along the way that may be a little out of the ordinary. Romance is flowers sometimes; an occasional gift for no reason; a phone call just to say "I love you"; a surprise note found in a lunch box or a pocket; a weekend away alone together; a spontaneous picnic on Sunday afternoon ....

In other words, care enough about each other to want to make your partner happy. We are not telling you that it is necessarily an easy thing to keep romance alive in view of the frantic lives we all seem to live today, but we are saying that it is necessary to a happy and healthy relationship. All of these little thoughtful things contribute, over a period of time, to making the other person feel loved, and a feeling of being loved is the biggest thing that keeps a relationship alive.

This isn't a "boy or girl" thing. It is a two-way street and both parties bear responsibility for finding ways to keep love alive. So take a chance, do something different and have fun!

# 4

## THE NEED FOR FREEDOM
## WITHIN A RELATIONSHIP

Each of us comes to planet Earth as a very special soul, whole and complete just the way we are. Within a relationship, it is necessary for both partners to appreciate each other "just the way they are." That means trusting each other and letting go of our built-in urges to "control." It also means letting go of insecurities, feeling confident that your partner will always be there for you.

Each of us needs some time to ourselves and it is important in any relationship that both partners be allowed some "alone" time without one partner feeling guilty or the other feeling deprived.

"Clingy and needy" just don't work in a relationship! Clingy and needy are usually the result of insecurities, or control issues. Either way, it is a sure-fire way to strangle or smother the relationship. Allowing each other time to breathe, reflect, meditate or just read the paper quietly, refreshes the spirit and brings renewed energy and harmony to a relationship.

*Be yourself. Look in the mirror and love who you are.*

# 5

## Forgiveness

When all else fails, forgiveness may be the only solution. Forgiveness may be the only reason a relationship remains intact. Every relationship involves give and take and every relationship is bound to involve a need for one party to forgive the other somewhere along the line. If you recognize your own shortcomings, you will find it easier to forgive someone else's shortcomings.

You can't change the past and regrets are a waste of time. We have all had our share of regrets, and they haven't changed anything. All you can do is accept where you are, and move on. Put resentment behind you if you ever want to find peace and happiness.

*If you can't forgive, it is like holding a hot coal in your hand—you are the one getting burned!*

## 6

### LIVING ALONE AND LIKING IT

When you have come to the conclusion that your relationship is over, and you have removed yourself from the situation, you will have choices to make. Here is the way we see it.

**One:** You can jump right back into another relationship (probably with the same results).
**Two:** You can take a two-year sabbatical from relationships while you look at where you have been (this is necessary if you don't want to make the same mistakes again).
**Three:** You can take the time to figure out what you really want in your life.
**Four:** You can decide whether you want to have a partner in your life or you want to be alone.

Most people think they don't want to be alone. "Alone" is a scary word, especially if you have been in a relationship for a long time. However, if you have taken the two-year sabbatical (which we heartily suggest!), you may have figured out whether you want to have a partner or you would like to spend some time alone. Instead of thinking of yourself as being alone, think of yourself as being "independent"!

Living alone "forever" may not be the answer for you. But allowing yourself to be alone for a while, and not being afraid to do so, could make a huge difference in the kind of relationship you create for yourself in the future.

## FINALLY...

It is our hope that we have given you some ideas, some solutions and the strength to use them in your relationships. Always remember you are not alone in your experiences. You have many kindred spirits in this arena, ourselves included! Learning to live with each other in harmony is a huge lesson on planet Earth.

We wish you good luck and Godspeed in your relationship endeavors.

# HELPFUL HINTS FOR A LOVING RELATIONSHIP

1. Lust is blind and does not necessarily lead to lasting love.

2. Hasten slowly—a garden of real friends grows slowly. "Old fashioned" is not a bad thing.

3. "Live and let live"—a motto to guide everyone in relationships.

4. You must decide if it is more important to be "right" or to be "loved"!

5. Be willing to step "outside the box" when creating what you consider a "good" relationship.

6. Choose to focus only on the positive aspects of your friends and partner.

7. When faced with what is seemingly a huge problem, choose to be solution-oriented.

8. Listen to others with your heart, and ask yourself how the other person is being a mirror for you.

9. Be willing to let go of the past, because what matters is NOW.

10. Always remember to give an encouraging word, even if you think the other person is not "deserving" of it.

11. Learn to accept people as they are, not as you wish they would be.

12. Moving on is hard to do, but the ability to do it, when necessary, puts you on a positive path to a good relationship.

13. "Alone" is not a dirty word. Time alone leads to introspection and learning about 1/2 of any relationship—YOU!

14. We live in a time that operates at warp speed and that is not necessarily great for relationships. Take time to stop and smell the roses—together!

Breinigsville, PA USA
11 March 2011
257474BV00001B/2/P